KIDS TENNIS

MINI PLAYERS

GUIDELINES FOR TEACHING AND LEARNING

MAKE IT CREATIVE, FUN, DYNAMIC

Martín Rocca Josep Campos-Rius

About the authors:

Martin Rocca

Tennis Coach Level 1-2 (Argentina), USPTR *coach* (USA), Tennis Coach Level 1 , Aflilated RPT Coach (Spain).
Certified Tournament Official, Sports Director by the Catalan Tennis Federation, Wheelchair Tennis Coach for the Spanish Tennis Federation.
Mini Players Director and *TennisAid* Co-Founder.
RFET member of the Coaches Education and Research Department.
Coach the Coaches-Kids Tennis Conference speaker and member.
Coaching staff for the Bepro Deporte España Foundation..
Conference speaker. Wilson Tennis ambassador in Spain
Real Club de Tennis Barcelona 1899 tennis coach.

Twitter: @miniplayers10 | @10martinrocca | @TennisAid1
Instagram: @miniplayers10 | @10martinrocca | @TennisAid1
Facebook: Martín Rocca
Linkedin: linkedin.com/in/martinroccatenniscoach
E-mail: miniplayers10@gmail.com

Josep Campos-Rius

Graduate in Physical Education from INEFC Barcelona (University of Barcelona).

PhD in Sport Sciences. Doctoral thesis: "The professional competences of the tennis coach. The vision of their trainers at international level".

National Tennis Coach.

Director of Training and Research Department of the Catalan Tennis Federation from 2005 to 2015.

University professor since 2002. General coordinator and coordinator Official master in training Teachers for Secondary and Sixth-Form Teaching, Vocational Training and Language Teaching at the FPCEE Blanquerna-Universitat Ramon Llull since 2018.

Tennis expert at i-Coach of the International Tennis Federation.

Lecturer in the master's degree in Performance Analysis, Innovation and Development in Tennis (MEDAC - Official Institute of Vocational Training).

Trainer at Vibliotec.org (Sports Knowledge Community).

Specialist in Tennis Teaching and Training Methodology and Physical Education and Sport Didactics.

Twitter: @JosepCampos_PhD
Instagram: @josep_campos_rius
Facebook: Josep Campos
Linkedin: linkedin.com/in/josepcamposrius
E-mail: josepcampos@gmail.com

#TennisFriends

Lara Arruabarrena –WTA Professional player

To me, it is crucial what you do with little kids because it´s when you grab the racket djfot the fist time, you get to know the first moves on the court and you start learning the things you will improve as you get older. That´s why I think, coaches in this area should be good professionals and well prepared. This is fundamental in tennis.

Conchita Martínez – Former Wimbledon champion

When it comes to teaching tennis and on the other side of the net there are young kids, the figure of a good coach becomes more relevant. A qualified coach will allow the kids to improve on skills, motivation and love for the game and to maximize their potential during the teaching-learning process to get the best of their abilities.

Judy Murray – Tennis Coach. Former Fed Cup Team GB Captain. *Miss Hits-She Rallies-Tennis on the Road-Judy Murray Foundation*

Tennis is competing with so many other sports and leisure activities for people´s time nowadays that it´s crucial that we create fun and stimulating learning environments in which kids, teens and adults can thrive. Such environments are always brought to life by people. People who understand the game and catter for the different ages, stages and backgrounds of the customers in front of them. One size never fits all.
Martín Rocca has over 30 years of tennis teaching experience and his love of the game is second to none. He has packaged his philosophy and his extensive content into 130+ pages with colourful illustrations and links to video clips. This s a "must have" for coaches and parents.

Romina Puglia – Develpoment area Director (Argentinian Tennis Association). Creator of Gen10s y Red en Juego Programmes. Jugando Hacia el Futuro Foundation President.

It is not an easy task for me to write about the impact this book can have on readers as it is an open door for new concepts and ideas about teaching kids. For a few years now, I have seen in Martin´s work a reflection of my ideals in terms of introducing young players into the game, a path where intrigue, attention and time lead a way to get involved in a game no matter the social, economical or cultural contexts.
I hope and I wish everyone can enjoy what Martin and Josep are offering us in this book, with such generosity to have more methodogical tools to teach our kids.

In this book we will see thet way this philosophy has been implemented in many countries, under a wide range of different environments, possibilities and needs and help in the development of motor skills, abilities, social interaction and team-building mentality.

Mini Players develops a way of coaching that can be applied no matter where you are, a club, a field with no equipement, a primary school yard, etc. So all kids and teens from Uganda, Spain, Argentina and more, can learn this sport having Mini Players as an universal language.

Carla Suárez – WTA Profesional player

As I see tennis, the beginning is a crucial moment. The first momento you connect with the sport has to be special. When a kid is learning to play the game, technique, positioning, mobility, are extremely important to hit the ball well and to prevent future injuries. All of that is going to affect directly the evolution of a player. Having a strong base it is important. I think in Spain we should pay more attention to this stage because it is the one that builds players with good capacities.
To me, a coach that is working with professional players on tour or a coach that is teaching kids in a club have the same relevance.
Little kids deserve coaches with integrity and a professional approach to them.
The target should be having kids enjoying their sessions, coming to the club with a smile on their faces, joining a group of friends and challenging themselves to improve their game.
Coaches must understand that facing these stages require serious work and qualification.
I want to thank all the coaches who dedicate their profesional life to teach the sport to newcomers and youngsters and for showing a way to enjoy this sport. All of us who make a leaving out of playing tennis are extremely thankful for their love and dedication.

Severine Tamborero – Tennis coach. Author. Conference speaker. U-10 tennis programme Director forTennis Canada

Martín has been coaching for the past 30 years. He is passionate about kids and wants the best for them on and off the court.
Martin´s experience bring so much for our sport and for our profession.
There are a lot of experience and knowledge behind this book and like his coaching, it is done from the heart. Very proud of you, Martin!!

Emma Wells - *Wimbledon Park Tennis Director*

Martin´s passion and innovation for kids tennis is a whole new level. Martin makes learning fun and progressive. His knowledge and ideas are recognized aroud the world and will continue to evolve with this incredible book.

Pancho Alvariño – Pancho Alvariño Academy Director. ITF Expert. Former Spanish Fed-Cup captain.

I feel privileged to reccomend this book that finally sees the light. Martin is not only a colleague but also a good friend. He studied, experimented and researched a lot in many different places to create Mini Players, which reflects his persona, the passion for teaching and love for this profession. A very useful guide for coaches, a methodology that basically teaches trhough the game, provides a huge ammount of tools to apply during the teaching-learning process with kids.

Jordi Arrese – Former Professional Player and Davis Cup Captain. Silver medalist at the Barcelona ´92 Summer Olympics

In this book, Martin and Josep provide the tools to use during the teaching process in early stages based on knowledge and experience. By reading it, you will have a global vision and a number of ideas to help you in your daily sessions. I hope coaches find this book attractive and useful, especially those who are working with young kids.

Miguel Crespo – PhD. RFET Professor. ITF.

Helping young people to play the sport is fundamental for the future of tennis. Doing so requires passion, dedication, but also qualification and experience. The authors, who have many years in this business, have made this manual combining fun and creativity. I want to congratulate them for sharing their visión and also ask coaches to enjoy their reading and try to apply the many ideas that, for sure, they will find here to improve their programmes.

Jofre Porta –*Global Tennis Team* Director. Former coach of Rafael Nadal and Carlos Moyà. Conference speaker.

We, the people who believe that sports are an educating weapon, will feel very happy with this book. The recreational tennis has an important effect on players formation both for the sport and life itself.
The Martin-Josep combination brings quality and this book will be a good balance between the traditional and the technological, the theory and the practical execution.
This book will have to be always near he courts and I don´t think I have to wish you luck with it because you won´t need it, it will be a success for sure.

David Sanz Rivas – Sports Science Phd. RFET Professor. RFET Educationd and Research Director (September 2003 - March 2020)

The first stages in tennis are really important, not only because they will build a solid structure for a future tennis player, no matter the level of skills, but because of the way they would assimilate concepts, they will have a progress into the sport. .

Ths book offers this kind of approach based on learning through the game, evolving in a systematic and progressive way that allow learning in a natural manner, that's why the authors are recognized personalities in this area. I'm convinced this will be a referencial and helpful tool to use with kids that are taking their first steps into our sport.

Pepe Vendrell – *Coach* ATP. Roberto Bautista Agut team.

Working professionally with little kids is authentic and honest. There are no filters, it's the beginning of everything, where it all starts, where a coach gets passionate about this profession. This is the first and best step we can take, enjoy the ride.

DEDICATED TO:

Being my first book, I want to dedícate it to the people that got me involved into the tennis world.

To Guillermo Vilas, for being the beginning of everything
To Jorge Cuska (Buenos Aires), for giving me space with freedom
To Xavier Luna (New York), for teaching me what passion means
To Ramon Capdevila (Reus), for his professional dedication
And in the end, to all coaches who dignify this profession
Special thanks to Laura Partal and to my friend Josep Campos-Rius

Martín Rocca

To the girls and boys who learn and enjoy the sport
To the families who bring their kids to us to show them a path into the sport
To the coaches who make tennis, the best sport in the world
To Martin Rocca, for his energy and passion

Josep Campos-Rius.

Index

Foreword

To me it is a great honour and a privilege to write this foreword for "Kids Tennis- MINI PLAYERS: Guidelines for teaching and learning" from Josep and Martin, two good friends. We are talking about two professionals that combine teaching with passion on one side, and the understanding of the glogal game and the ways to properly showcase it on the other.

By Reading this book, you will be able to recognise how to teach the sport from equipment familiarisation to the acquisition of more complicated moves and techniques. And all of these with an open methodology that was build based on experiences from coaches and clubs form all over the world.

You will also be able to get into a methodology that teaches through a fun environment, that promotes experimentation and creativity putting the focus on the players to make them love the sport for the rest of their lives. When I look back and I remember my first contact with tennis, joy and nostalgy come to my mind for having a group of friends with similar goals and coaches who were working hard to make as feel at home and to create something that would last for a long time. I have tried to keep those emotions and feelings alive during my entire professional carrer. I´m convinced the first stages in tennis have to be well taken care of and conceive them as the most important, no unnecesary pressures and make sure, girls and boys can understand what we can expect from them according to their possibilities to avoid frustrations and, eventually, kids leaving the sport.

Besides the methodologies that Martin and Josep are sharing with us, you will also have the chance to learn tennis from a different approach, by helping others to get connected to the sport like *Tennis Aid* does and, in the end, see that tennis is a way to learn on good values off the court too. You will learn how to win, lose, listen and so many more things that will help you in your personal and professional life by having an open mind.
Tennis is a school for life. Don´t miss out this opportunity!

I encourage you to read this book and recognise the effort the authors have made to show their love and passion for teaching and I congratulate them for doing so.

My best regards to the tennis world, enjoy the reading!

Àlex Corretja

Former Professional Tennis Player

Introduction

Working with kids is far more complicated than you think but at the same time, it is easier than you can imagine.

Why is it more complicated?

Because we are talking about teaching a sport to very young people without a deep knowledge of their own bodies and possibilities and to do so it is recurrent to see inexperienced personal in charge of their sessions. In many occasions, the final target it is confused with having a fun environment but with a lack of real content.

The FUN factor shold **always** be present while teaching girls and boys, but it is **essencial** that everything we do with them, would help them to improve their skills and understand the game. That is why, coaches in charge of these groups should always be qualified and in case of having young coaches, they should have a more experienced guide by their side.

And why is it easier that we can imagine?

The answer is simple if you know what to do and when. Letort (2002), said a kid is by no means an adult in a smaller scale. Having that in mind, we can have a huge range of possibilities to work with kids.

The biggest challenge that still persists in many clubs and coaches´ mentality is the idea of teaching technique from minute one. This means that the first thing a coach will teach is to position a kid to hit forehands and backhands. It is a noble idea but not the proper one.

It is important to remember the obstacles we find in the way during these stages as Martínez (2000) points out in the Sports Initiation Manual for Coaches:

- Non-qualified staffers.
- Excessive technical/tactical instructions.
- Results oriented mentality.
- Lack of plannification.
- Imitation of professional models.

If we think about a boy or a girl that comes to the court for the first time, we should consider the obvious fact that they want to PLAY. We are not talking about playing a real match, but getting involed ina fun, collective activity. Nonetheless, what usually happens is that the kids receive a large list of instructions:

- How to position their body (that they still don´t dominate).
- How to grab/place the racket (that they don´t know how to handle).
- How to hit a ball (that they will have to find in the air without previos preparation for it).
- And, to finish it off and to make it even more dificult, to follow through.

So the big question marks all of these things are generating are:

- Is this the right methidology?
- Is this fun?

- Is there any room for kids´ creativity to freely use rackets and balls to get used to them or they only have to follow technical instructions?

Our **proposal** is that we can have a different vision to face this wonderful challenge.
First of all, we need to recognise the motor capabilities of our young players, we have to know what type of language we must use, for how long we have to talk to them, what kind of abilities and skills we can work with them for a better development and to avoid frustrations.
Goodway, Ozmun & Gallahue (2019) proposed orientations to have in mind when it comes to players in development ages:

- At a **cognitive** level, the power of creativity and imagnation the kids already have, the ability to express themselves and their will for discovery.
- At the **afective** level, they mention their ego and fear of frustrations.
- About **physical and motor development** they talk about kids getting tired too qickly, slow growth, but by the time they are 8-9 years old they have a visual perception fully developed and a bigger motor control of basic abilities.

After all these arguments, it would be easy to understand that if we place a number of kids in a long line to wait for the moment to hit a ball, that won´t be extremely attractive to them.
The will of this book is to **propose** methodological orientations and basic didactics to simplify the training of young players and allow them to be introduced in this wonderful sport and learn how to practice it and play it in a fun and effective way.
For instance, aswering questions like:

- Do you think you can run a lesson without feeding balls from a basket?
- Do you think you can teach without a basket/cart?
- Do you think you could teach with only one ball per kid the entire session?

WEll, this can be done and we´ll try to explain how. From game oriented excercises, to the understanding of the game and away from traditional methods based on the repetition of mechanics.
Kids should be constantly moving doing activities that engage them at a motor and cognitive level and everything they do, has to be oriented to a future technical gesture. This is why we have to work with them to improve their motor skills, their spatial awareness, the meaning of teamwork, to respect coaches indications and also to understand what to do every time they hit a ball, to comprehend the sport in a simple and fun way.

Every ball has a purpose and a destination

This is the base of this philosophy. When a kid hits a lot of balls in a sequence, the focus is on the technical gesture. But if every ball that is hit goes back to the coach, to a certain zone on the court, to another kid who is waiting for that ball to catch it with a cone, with his/her hands, stop it with a racket or simply hit it back, that ball not only will have a very useful destination; by doing that, the kid will control directions, the amount of power needed to reach a goal and eventually to get ready to get that ball back. So, from the very beginning, we are helping the kid to understand what it means to hit a ball and be aware when it comes back.

How to work with little kids

Foam ball stage

Very interesting stage, for sure. Kids are coming to see what this sport can offer them and a huge range of possibilities gets in front of their eyes and we coaches, have a great responsibility to show them what this sport can bring to their lives and to use their imagination and creativity in the process.

It is important to understand that the racket won´t be the only tool the kids will have. It´s going to be another piece of the puzzle to introduce them into tennis. The most relevant tool is their own body and we have to teach them to maximise their potential.

Teaching abilities like running, jumping, throwing, rolling, catching must be a priority. A kid able to dominate all of those abilities will be much better than others with a racket in hand.

In this stage, Temple & O'Connor (2005) suggest the need of developing motor skills in kids for the impact they will have when they get older. About this, if the fundamentals are tought correctly, they will have an important rol on getting more self-efficient players.

Involving kids in different activities is ideal and using adapted equipment is always an entertaining but useful way to reach good goals.

You can introduce different coordination sessions to improve a number of skills. Using motricity tracks allow coaches to have various kids in a session, all active, working separate abilities.

Tracks can involve, running, jumping, changing directions, side steps. Others when kids are throwing and catching. By doing rotations, kids can work many different abilities in one dynamic session.

In these situations, a coach must be a guide proposing activities and challenging the kids to make them the best way they can instead of saying that there is only one way to do them.

Being so young, they will make a lot of mistakes, they will get confused, will lose their balance, and the coach must be aware of that, paying attention to safety and not exceed in a lot of instructions.

Both coaches and players should be enjoying every minute of it.

Communication is key.
The level of empathy with kids is crucial and having clear goals will make this process fun and effective.

First steps for mini-tennis players

Red ball stage

Once the kids have passed the first stage, where they got in touch with the court, all types of materials used in the sessions, they know the environment and dominate theirs bodies better, we dive into a group with great potential for learning and improvement.

Our goals would be successful if by the end of this stage, kids are able to rally by themselves, and if they get to know the basic technical displacements and tactical idea of the game.

Just like the previous stage, technical requirements are not that necessary, as Muñoz, García, Timón, Olcina (2006) suggest by saying "base this process on the comprehension of the game over playful, recreational principles, away from technical approaches".

It is recommended to work in small areas, so the ful length of a swing it is not fully necessary. Dominating the contact point would give them what they need and that would allow them to start playing.

If a kid i sable to hit the ball back to the coach or a teammate in a right way and keep an exchange under control we could consider that this particular gesture, only focused on the contact, it is the right one at this particular moment.

If we put a lot of emphasis on the follow through (very common to see coaches doing this) we are not focusing on the correct priorities. If a kid is thinking about finishing the rackets over the shoulder, will not be paying attention to the contact point. This also happen when coaches teach drills with lots of repetitions. Kids must finish a gesture, but, as we mentioned earlier they are not payin attention to the ball´s destination, that means, more complicated technique and no exchanges (rallies) at sight.

It is hard to estipulate concrete technical parameters or program long-term working sequences when you deal with so many intangibles as in a tennis group. For instance, PE class at a primary school will have the same number of kids throughout the year with very little or no variations at all.

But in tennis, this could be affected by a big number of circumstances, given the fact that in the middle of the season, a kid who is performing well could be promoted to a better group, new kids can join your programme well after the season started, there are times when kids miss a lot of sessions (skiing family time!).

Facing all these factors, it´s not easy to follow a well detailed programming because you have to constantly adjust to changes year after year, even though the general goals can be similar, that´s why it is important to **adapt** your sessions to the group´s possibilities and be open minded about it.

That being said, it is relevant to understand where do we set up a finish line to them. The red ball stage is the first one where we have to make our kids feel that they are (little) tennis players in the making.

They get attracted and motivated by team tasks rather than individual ones, so most of the activities should be focused on cooperation and collaboration. The dynamics of sessions should be high, keeping kids active and participative and, at the same time, generating a bonding spirit of camaraderie.

A coach should guide them without the use of technical language, trying to be a mediator, a link between players and tasks. Someone **suggesting** how to do something instead of demanding it.

The number of shots practiced on each excercise won´t have to include too many repetitions. Sometimes it is much better to do 1 or 2 shots with full attention than doing a big number of hits with a lack of quality in the execution. Their concentration span is too short, so if we ask them so do something brief, they will perform better.

Less shots + full focus + positive *feedback*

=

EXCELLENT RESULTS

To have in mind

In these two groups (foam-red), the coach´s figure changes completely compared to the more traditional models. If in the first one, the focus is more on motricity and basic skill-building tasks and in Red, the kids start taking their first steps into playing, **it would be almost unnecessary for a coach to use a racket during these periods.** A coach would be more a session coordinator than a ball feeder.

Orange ball stage

We are getting serious

If the progression of the previous groups was accurate, we get to a point where kids can play with own serve (underhanded), they keep a consistent rally and play points with a basic tactical idea.

If we consider that this stage would last 2 seasons (between 6-9 years old aprox), we should get players with a good contact point and we´ll have to focus on a longer swing now.

Now they will start playing in a slightly bigger court, so they will need to swing the racket differently. **So the first thing we´ll add is the follow through**. A longer racket motion will give them the depth they need without the use of more power. The coach should put emphasis now on the lenght of the swing.

Just by mentioning that they need to hit the ball deeper, kids will start making adjustments to get the job done.

Why not working the Backswing first?

Because, even though they changed groups and they play on a bigger court, it is still a reduced area In fact, it is recommendable to keep on working at close range to maintain the ball and movement control.

Focusing the attention on a backswing would variate the racket motion, and that would affect the ball control.

The orange phase becomes more technical, footwork takes a bigger relevance with more complicated excercises, always paying good attention to balance. If players can´t control their postures when running, stopping and hitting, we should insist on those factors instead of moving forward. **All activities made by players in reduced areas and slow speed, allow them to control their bodies, be more efficient and understand every move much better.** (Mowling & Heidorn, 2013).

How should we train the orange ball players?

At this point, kids usually have an important level of self-steem and confidence. This is no new territory for them. They feel they can play, so we have to start coaching them to shape their strokes and moves and increase the level of difficulties to help them perform efficiently. Introduction of volley progressions (if you haven´t done a lot with them in the red ball group) and serve are crucial here.

We don´t have to fall in the common mistake of teaching them alternative grips to eventually correct them in the future because they create bad habits that are very difficult to erase and modify as kids get older.

Continental grip progressions are a safe investment. Kids have remarkable adptability and flexibility, so learning this grip shouldn´t be that hard.

One of the biggest problems we face in these ages are how fast we demand results. If a player gets the serve in by just tapping it with an Eastern grip, that boy or gilr will be playing tournaments immediately. **We consider this, a big mistake.**

There is no need for kids to jump over stages. Doing routine racket-handling games to get used to this grip would help strengthening the wrist and get to pronate by playing fun games like bouncing the ball off the frame, so by the time they practice volleys and serves, they have a more natural feeling about the racket.

Tactical concepts should intensify here because kids´ perception is much wider and they can analyse and process decision making moments better.

Following this path, the introduction to effects and special shots (sliced backhands, drop-shots, etc) should be consider to increase the possibilities in our players repertoire.

Coaching these kids, at this age when they are much more conscious about themselves and the game, sessions can be organized to work on their authonomy and allow them to make their own decisions.

Avilés, Campos y Abarca (1996) propossed methodological orientations metodológicas by doing:

- Exchanges between players and coaches.
- Exchanges between players with the assist of a coach.
- Exchanges between players.
- Hitting againtst a wall.
- Using obstacle tracks and stations.

Same authors suggest that the most appropriate teaching styles would be mutual teaching (cooperation), tasks assignments, guided discovery and problems resolutions.

The focus on technique

Green ball stage

Once we arived to this group, the technical level of our players should be important. Nevertheless, we will work here every move to the detail, every type of footwork; we will coach based more on repetitions, unlike the previous groups to make sure they have a solid base. There will be much more competition between players and we´ll focus more attention on strategy, technique, tactical decisions and rules to prepared them to tournament play accordingly.

To have better numbers on efficient playing it is vital to be in good position prior hitting. So, footwork will be massively relevant here.

A player with good shots will lack efficiency if those shots are hit in bad positioning or balance. We must insist on concentration, movement, reaction speed, knees bent, adjustment steps to make sure they all are in the right place at the right time to hit correctly.

What happens when a green ball player has a very good level?

A very common mistake: Getting these kids to play with **yellow balls**. These are some arguments about it:

-   They are ready to play on full court.
-   So they get used to yellow balls.
-   So they can play some U-12 tournaments.

Using low-compression balls has a positive effect on shots develpoment. The power appiled without hitting the ball out (beyond the baseline) makes rallies more consistent and gives players a sense of confidence. (Hammond & Smith, 2006). Also, Kachel, Buszard & Reid (2015) they mention that contact point is improved, reinforces the technique and prevents injuries.

Two players rallying both with yellow and green balls will have a more efficient exchange with a softer ball.

In this stage we must pay special attention to the introduction to competition. This will be the last phase with transition balls and as it happens very often kids get involved in tournaments using yellow balls, when they are not used to them. The rythm of rallying increases and that will directly affect the technique, not respeting all the previous work done with these players in the recent years. This is why we suggest to maximise the use of green balls to make sure the players have more control over their actions.

Coyle (2012) said: "If you have early success, ignore the praise and try to reach the best of your possibilities. If you don´t find success, don´t quit. **Your efforts must be valued as experiments, not as veredicts**. This is a marathon, not a sprint".

In many ocassions we find U-10 players having good results, being much better than the rest for having more technical quality, for anthropometry or power. They get used to winning with no effort, which can lead to many problems in the future:

- Generating false expectations on parents, coaches and own players.
- Thinking that they don´t need to train hard because, as the results show, they win easily by doing very little.
- Not undesrstanding that at this age, most rivals are tottaly unexperienced players, something that is **not going to happen** in following categories.
- Early burn-out after too many turnaments and training sessions.

To avoid this, a coach should teach his/her players to mantain a high level of compromise on each session. At this level, coaches need to provide real, sincere feedback, reward effort, let everone have a voice and presence (not only the most skillful ones) and value performance and not results (Martínez, 2010).

Mini Players Philosophy

Kids tennis
Development of young tennis players

Guidelines to work with kids
based on discovery,
imagination and motor skills.

Sessions must be adapted to equipment and facilities that we have. They can go from a regular tennis club, a school yard or a multi-sports area.
Also adapt to the number of kids and their level of skills.
Respect this philosophy: Go slow. Go from low to high with no hurries.

Philosophy principles

You can start teaching 3-year-old kids by following this principle: Purely technical concepts shouldn´t be used at this ages. Kids should face all sort of situations and discover which is the right option for them. They must face challenges that are close to their capabilities.
Big focus on motricity and emphasis on movement and hand throwing.

Session dynamics

Kids should learn to respect an order of sequences in our progressions, they have to be in constant action and there are **NO LINES.**

You can easily have 8-10 players on a court (coach + assistant).
Highly recommended to keep them in constant motion; technical language is not necessary, use simple and short instructions and watch for safety measures, controlling the distance between kids to avoid accidents.

Equipment and space needed

Using adapted equipment should be absolutely out of question.
It is advised to use colourful, diverse materials to make the playing field more enjoyable and fruitful at the same time.

Equipment

If you have the chance of using materials such as steps, bosus, hoops, bricks, sticks, etc., the possibilities of running a good motricity session and fun all at once are endless. They help our players to improve their motor skills if we don´t only focus on teaching how to reproduce a technical gesture.

There are so many different items that can help you lead a dynamic session, visually more atractive, but also useful.

Nonetheless, all of these tools can only be part of the process. By no means, they should monopolize the organisation of the sessions.

Paddles, rackets, balls: They are facilitators. Much needed.

Rebo Wall: Ball control with a wide range of possibilities.

Top Spin Pro: A great tool to learn the use of spins.

Serve Master: Provides a fluid service motion.

Leds React: So many different options to work on reaction, decision making...

Backswing Solution: Eliminates unnecessary arm-racket motion.

SVTA: Visual training easy to adapt anywhere with any groups.

Balls

<u>Baby Ball</u>: ideal for the yonger ones, to plat floor tennis and work from day one on ball tracking.

<u>Foam ball</u>: slightly bigger than conventional balls, are extremely light. They provide a soft impact and a very low bounce

<u>Red ball</u>: they make the first rallies much easier with only a 25% of pressure.

Orange ball: regular size, this ball provides a good bounce and it is the one that help the players shape their strokes. (50% pressure).

Green ball: last stop for kids before they jump into conventional yellow balls. (75%)

Yellow ball: Conventional ball used by kids and adults.

Courts

<u>Red court</u>: you can make 4 to 6 red ball tennis courts on a conventional one by setting up mini tennis nets and turning side lines into baselines.

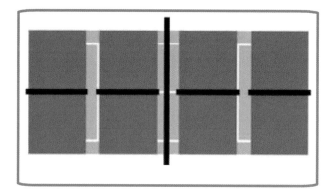

<u>Orange court</u>: a rectangle inside a conventional court.

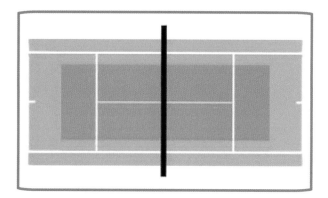

<u>Green court</u>: a full conventional court.

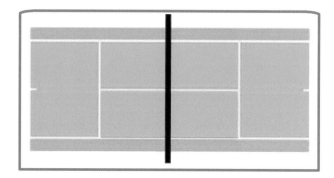

Programmes and methodologies

Here we present different programmes ran by federations, that provide their particular vision on how to teach and promote tennis.

INTERNATIONAL TENNIS FEDERATION (ITF): *Play and Stay.*

TENNIS AUSTRALIA-NEW ZEALAND: Hot Shots.

LAWN TENNIS ASSOCIATION (LTA): *Tennis for Kids.*

UNITED STATES TENNIS ASSOCIATION **(USTA)***: Net Generation.*

REAL FEDERACIÓN ESPAÑOLA DE TENIS (RFET): Tenis X Etapas.

ASOCIACIÓN ARGENTINA DE TENIS (AAT): GEN10'S

FÉDÉRATION FRANÇAISE DE TENNIS (FFT): Galaxie Tennis

Other methodologies and systems

System 9 (Andy Dowsett)

Divertitenis (Horacio Rodríguez Molaro)

MissHits (Judy Murray)

Evolution Kids Tennis (Mike Barrell)

Inspire2Coach (Mark Tennant & Richard Marklow)

Alternative scoring and competition formats

IPTL (Steve Chiu)

THIRTY30 (Mark Milne)

UTR (Universal Tennis Rating)

Mini Players. How does it work?

In this chapter we propose methodological orientations according to the stage, kids age and their skill level.

3-6 year old

- Foam and red balls.
- Little use of rackets in the beginning of the session.
- Coordination of movement and ball throwing.
- Learning of working habits and session´s dynamics.
- Constant activity, teamwork multiple and simple goals.

6-8 years old

- Progression from red to orange balls.
- First techical concepts in terms of backswing and follow-through.
- Always working at very close range.
- Ball control, a priority.

9-10 years old

- Continue with orange balls until group level can handle green balls.
- Use orange ball court size to keep on improving the all-around game.
- Ball control rather than power.
- Not all kids can play full court at this stage.

Motricity tracks

Formats change according to kids' level of skills. Must be original, colourful but above all, useful. They must fulfil specific functions and help develope different abilities.

Mini Players special touch

- No lines.
- No use of ball feeding and mechanization by repetitions.
- Big number of kids on one court but always in continuous motion.
- **You can run a session with only one ball per kid**.

Taking care of equipment

As coaches, we have to teach the kids to respect, protect and give good use to all type of pieces of equipment used during training.
Careless usage will lead to broken or lost pieces that would have to be replaced, but also it is a demonstration that a group is not being controlled correctly by the coach.

Equipment collection

At the end of playing time, the equipment should be picked-up by the same players, always taking care of manners and safety measures.

Cooperation

The coach will assign a mission to every kid: "Please, pick up the cones"…
This will have the kids working even after the technical part of the session it´s done.
Make everyone feel that they are part of a team.
Congratulate them for doing the job correctly and in time. Little gestures usually have a great impact on our players. Keep this in mind.

Sessions orientation

3-6 years old: Exploration stage

- Begin with a lot of movement and no rackets.
- Teach them to throw-roll balls with both hands (*floorball*)
- With balls on the ground, ask them to tap them with the racket towards targets.
- Introduce bounce and self (underhanded) serve.
- If possible, ask them to bounce the ball and hit it softly towards the net.
- No power needed. Don´t let them hit the ball hard.
- Set up targets at close range.
- Introduce exchanges with no net.

7-8 years old: Global gesture

- Proper racket preparation-finish starting from ready position.
- Progressively introduce more complex footwork. Go slow!
- Movement should be taught correctly by going little by little. No need to rush.
- Rallies between players become more frequent and must be the base of trainings.
- Introduce the air game: Volleys, smash and progressions on serve.
- Point-playing on reduced areas.

9-10 years old: Shots and footwork specialization

- Special attention to movement, balance and positioning.
- Differentiation between defensive, neutral and attacking movement.
- Point-playing with full motion serve.
- Start by playing a lot of doubles matches and then move to singles. Analyse how the kids respond to that.
- Rallies and games only involving players. Coach acts as a moderator with sporadic interventions.

Introduction to competitions

Competition, in one way or another, must start early. It should be considered as part of the teaching-learning process. You can teach little kids to compete by following simple tasks:

- Who can hit the cones?
- How many different ways can you throw a ball?
- Who can run through the obstacle tracks without touching any elements?
- Which team can do more exchanges at toss and catch?
- Who can keep the longest rally with the coach?
- Adapt these goals to the kids´ possibilities. Try not to reward always the most skillful ones.

In the session

6-7 years olds can play points inside the service boxes. Underhanded serve.
To keep a high intense rotation, make them play only one point. Whoever wins the point stays on the winning side. Losers must go challenge players in other courts.
By playing this fast you avoid lines and teaches the kids the importance of concentrating point by point.
Fast doesn´t mean rush. Teach your kids to take their time before starting to play.

In tournaments

We recommend alternative scoring competitions. Round Robin formats so kids can play more. Not a good idea to send kids to play regular format tournaments (knock-out) without any experience.

- Mini tennis events
- Team competitions in small courts.
- Red, Orange, Green ball tournaments.
- Doubles.
- Friendly matches with other clubs. No unnecessary pressure due to ranking-related competition.

Sports-social values

The influence on kids behaviour; it is directly related to the sports learning process. It is absolutely necessary to teach them the value of words like teamwork, respect, discipline, sympathy, cooperation, joy, collaboration, etc.

It is the coach's responsibility to create a relaxed, disciplined and respectful training environment and setting the tone from the very beginning.

It is recommended to have all the kids working the same way, no hurries, but in constant motion under progressive patterns. Respect everyone´s style and the way they process the information.

.

Respect the players: make them feel like they belong in that place/team, let them have fun and show appreciation for their efforts.
Create a learning space where they feel free, autonomous.

Family role: families should be informed of everything we do with the kids and the have to understand their way to participate in this process. They are absolutely relevant, but all pieces of the puzzle (Parents, Kids, Coaches) must know their responsibilities and limitations.

Respect the coach: when a coach is talking, all kids should be silent and close to him/her. Instructions should be simple and brief. Don´t let kids bounce a ball or be distracted when talking to the group.

Promoting the sport

These are much needed actions in order to make your programme, club, sport grow. In order to be successful at them you need to be creative, compromised, dedicated and organized. You must facilitate the access to the sport to new people.

Different type of actions:

- Internal activities with your own players.
- Organize events with nearby clubs.
- Tennis in schools.
- Tennis on the street.
- Tennis in unusual places. (At a square, at any sporting event)

Special activities

You can involve players from all levels and ages:

- Red, orange and green ball kids, recreational players, competition players (even though they already have a lot of participation due to tournament play) and players of all ages.
- Invite non-members to come to the club (open door day), bring kids from primary schools in the area, invite people from foster care, institutions for people with special needs, senior citizens, etc.
- Special tournaments like father/mother-son/daughter challenge, best friends day, etc.

At the club

On the street

Emblematic places

In unusual areas

At local sporting events
Run an exhibition during a local sports encounter to show new audience what your kids are capable of doing That might attract new kids/families to visit your club.

Identification with the group

- Show kids why they are important for the group.
- Don´t reward only the skillful players.
- Always talk about the TEAM.
- Demand disciplne, respect and work ethic.
- Use a familiar langage to transmit tranquility and positive messages.
- Know the pros and cons of each player to try to get the best out of them.
- Create a commited, positive environment.

Tips

- EVERY kid is important. This should not be related to their skill level.
- If you organize events involving kids (as players, volunteers) ALL of them should have the chance to be part of.
- Select a player to lead the warm-up routine.

- When picking up balls, ALL players and coach should be involved. When you say: ¨Winners don´t pick up¨ you are sending a wrong message. That is part of the session and that includes everyone. Ball collection is not a punishment.

- Set up internal tournaments, set up friendly matches or trips with players who don´t usually compete.

- Praise punctuality, respect and team spirit from players who show that every day.
- Tell the little kids to bring their favourite toys to the court. They love sharing something that is a treasure for them.

Tennis and solidarity

- Sport promotion opens the door to a solidarity spirit.
- Make the sport accessible to those in need.
- Give all these kids the chance to play.
- Provide them (and their coaches) the necessary equipment to do the activity.

Dedication, love for the sport and the desire of seeing every kid having the chance to play should go hand in hand with your tennis programme.

We have a good example of this if we get to know **TennisAid**.

This is an association that promotes tennis around the world by providing equipment and technical assistance to coaches and players, especially in dissadvantaged areas.

It was created in 2014 by Abel Rincón and Martin Rocca in Barcelona, Spain.

After visiting Uganda in November 2014 and Cambodia in May 2015, the project continued it´s tireless work by helping local coaches to have the necessary equipment to teach kids in poor areas, providing proper gear and materials to young players with none or minimum budget to compete, to give an inmense number of kids clothes, shoes and rackets, promoting tennis programs for the disabled, etc.

How can a project like TennisAid affect your tennis programme?

Developing a solidarity spirit amongst your players takes the soul of the club to a higher level. Allows kids to value what they have, knowing that things they own and take for granted are much needed and appreciated in other areas.

What can a club do to be involved in a project like *TennisAid*?

You can ask all of your players-club members to donate the equipment they no longer use; run charity events to benefit a particular group-institution; sell merchandising products to collect funds.

Your club can sponsor a coach, an institution, a group and provide them funds or equipment periodically.

Another option it to promote tennis with an inclusive spirit, allowing the dissabled to play tennis in your club.

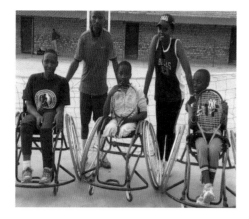 

Technical guide for coaches

Introduction

This is a working philosophy to teach kids in early stages that will help you to find the balance between:

- A purely technical, monotonous session.
- A very fun session but with no content.

These guidelines will provide ideas according to the different groups with excercises and video links.

We, the coaches, are here to educate and motivate and this book pretends to offer new ways of achieving that. By no means we are trying to imposse a working method; we are simply sharing experiences and methodological orientations that (hopefully) will help coaches do their job.

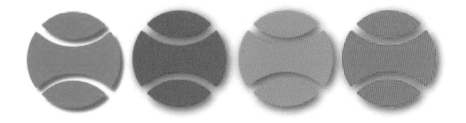

Respect evolutive stages

Adapted equipment

Teamwork

Ball control

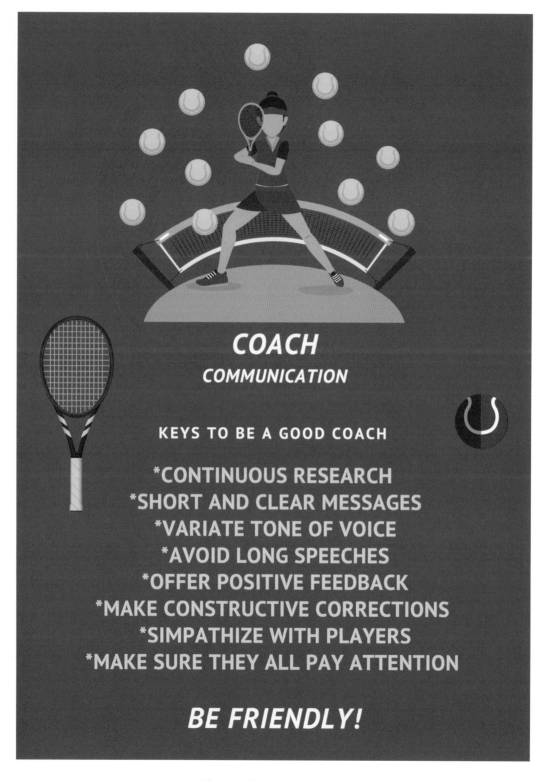

Keys to be a good coach

Foam ball stage

Youngest kids get into something completely new and experimentation and discovery are extremely important. Let´s show them what they can do with new tools, friends and a fun working place.

3 keys:

- First contact with the sport.
- Let the kids get used to the new environment, teammates, coaches and dynamics.
- Allow them to explore and create in a fun and festive zone.

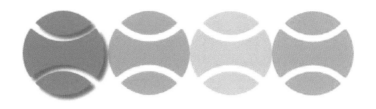

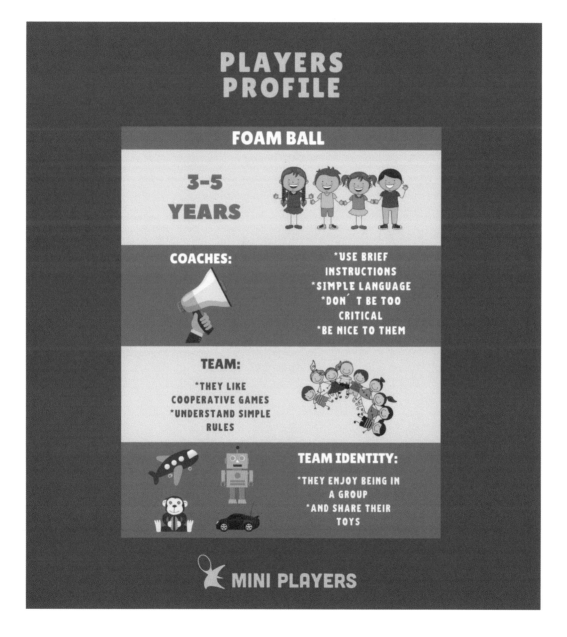

Foam ball stage
Warm-up

WE INTRODUCE KIDS INTO A NEW WORLD OF CHALLENGES AND ADVENTURES

DEVELOP MOTOR SKILLS AND THE USE OF NEW IMPLEMENTS TO MAKE THEM FEEL CONFIDENT

TRAIN THEIR MOTRICITY IN A FUN ENVIRONMENT ACCORDING TO THEIR OWN NEEDS AND POSSIBILITIES

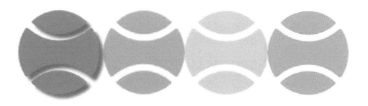

Foam ball stage
Warm-up

RUNNING THROUGH THE OBSTACLE TRACKS IS A GOOD WAY TO WARM-UP AND GET TO KNOW THE PLAYING AREA

RACKETS ARE NOT ALWAYS NECESSARY. MAKE THEM FIND DIFFERENT WAYS OF BEING ACTIVE

WALKING BACKWARDS, JUMPING, CRAWLING, RUNNING HOLDING HANDS WITH TEAMMATES. THEY ALL HELP TO IMPROVE MOVEMENT

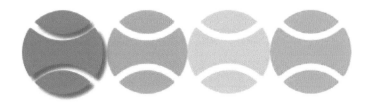

Foam ball stage
Activities

BALL THROWING WITH BOTH HANDS HELP THE KIDS TO WORK ON BOTH SIDES OF THE BODY AND CONTROL THE FUTURE RACKET SWING

USE DIFFERENT TRACKS DESIGNS TO INCREASE AND DEVELOP MORE CREATIVITY

LET´S TEACH THEM TO DOMINATE THEIR BODIES.
-JUMP AND CATCH
-JUMP AND TOSS
-JUMP AND RUN

Foam ball stage
Activities

PROGRESSIVE INTRODUCTION TO RACKET USE. HITTING BALLS SHOULD NOT BE THE ONLY TEACHING OPTION		
SIMPLE TARGETS WITH DYNAMIC ROUTINES. LET´S CHALLENGE THEM TO IMPROVE THEIR LEVEL OF ABILITIES		
FLOOR TENNIS. EASIEST WAY TO START EXCHANGES WITH PLAYERS		

  TIPS

1	**KEEP SAFETY MEASURES ALWAYS IN MIND**
2	**WATCH THE DISTANCE BETWEEN PLAYERS DURING ACTIVITIES**
3	**BE CAREFUL WHEN KIDS MANIPULATE RACKETS. AVOID ACCIDENTS**
4	**KIDS TRIP AND FALL VERY OFTEN. BE AWARE**

SAFETY FIRST

COACHES: KEEP YOUR EYES OPEN!

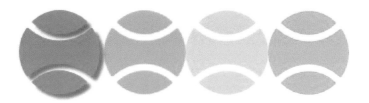

Foam ball stage
Conclusions

- Targets should be simple but with a practical meaning.
- Kids should learn to be part of a group, respecting coach, teammates, equipment and session´s dynamics.
- This stage should not be focused on ball hitting. This is not a technical phase.
- We are introducing kids in a new world, let them explore, discover and experiment new sensations.

Red ball stage

We keep on working on the development and improvement of abilities helping them to get to know better their bodies and the implements use.
The following 3 concepts are more important that mechanics:

- Freedom
- Exploration
- Creativity

Kids should learn how to recognize different types of actions according to their tasks, with implements like paddles, rackets, balls, etc., or without them.

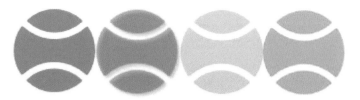

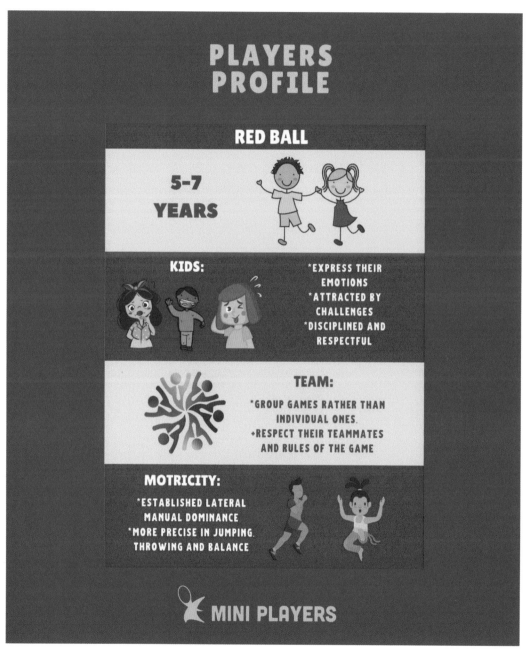

Red ball stage
Warm-up

RUNNING THE TRACKS AS TEAM COMPETITIONS BECOMES A MOTIVATING ACTIVITY

STROKES PROGRESSIONS AS PART OF THE WARM-UP ALLOW THE KIDS TO GET TO KNOW BETTER THE SHOT TO BE PRACTICED LATER ON

COLLECTIVE ACTIVITIES CREATE A TEAM SPIRIT. DON´T FOCUS ON INDIVIDUAL PERFORMANCE

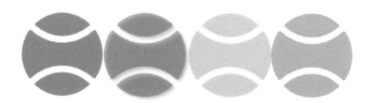

Red ball stage
Warm-up

CHALLENGE THE
KIDS TO DOMINATE
THEIR OWN SPACE,
IMPLEMENTS AND
ACHIEVE GOALS

BALL TRACKING.

WITH HANDS OR
IMPLEMENTS.
WITH OR WITHOUT
BOUNCE

GROUP TASKS.
TOSS AND CATCH.
TEAMWORK

Red ball stage
Activities

RECOMMENDED PROGRESSION:
*RUNNING THE TRACKS.
*THROW A BALL.
*PUSH IT WITH THE RACKET.
*HIT IT OVER THE NET

PUT THEIR SKILLS TO CHALLENGE IN A FESTIVE ENVIRONMENT. EASY TASKS CREATE A WRONG IDEA THAT WINNING NEEDS NO EFFORT

ENCOURAGE THEM TO DO THEIR OWN SERVE. THEY DON´T HAVE TO DEPEND ON BALL FEEDING

Red ball stage
Activities

WORKING IS SMALL AREAS IMPROVE BALL CONTROL		
PROPOSE PROGRESSIVE ACTIONS RESPECTING THE FUNDAMENTALS OF THE GAME.		
FIRST RALLIES OPEN A NEW CONCEPT FOR THEM AND THEY START FEELING LIKE REAL TENNIS PLAYERS		

Red ball stage
Activities

WE MUST GUIDE THEM BUT LET THEM DISCOVER THEY CAN DO THINGS ON THEIR OWN

DECISION MAKING. SOMETHING RARELY TRAINED AT THIS STAGES DUE TO LOADS OF INSTRUCTIONING

LET´S TEACH THEM EVERY SHOT WITH A PURPOSE AND MAKE IT THE BASE FOR THE FOLLOWING GOAL

MINIPLAYERS TIPS

HITTING THE BALL HARD IS UNNECESSARY

WORKING AT CLOSE RANGE IS RECOMMENDED

RUN A DYNAMIC AND STIMULATING SESSION

LOOK FOR KIDS TO CONTROL SPACE AND IMPLEMENTS

Red ball stage
Conclusions

- Training should be oriented to exchanges between players (floor tennis or exchanges without a net)
- In reduced áreas, kids must hit balls to coach´s hands. (control and direction)
- Contact point is the most important phase of the shot. Backswing and follow-through are not relevant now.
- Progressively move them from rallying without a net to a proper mini red court.

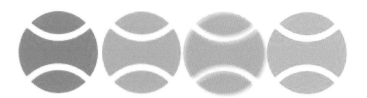

Orange ball stage

As court size increases, training incorporates the development of more specific gestures and mechanics and we propose a teaching-learning process based on play so kids can incorporate a proper global vision of the game.

2 keys to lead this process:

-   More emphasis on technical aspects both in shots and footwork
-   Tactical concepts gain more significance

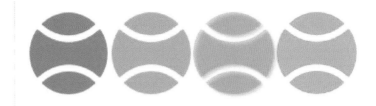

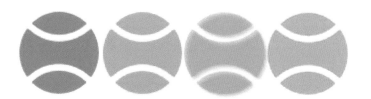

Orange ball stage
Warm-up

MOTRICITY TRACKS ARE STILL IMPORTANT TO IMPROVE IN FOOTWORK AND DECISION MAKING

REACTION AND COORDINATION GAMES

SPLIT-STEPS, CHANGE OF DIRECTIONS, BALANCE. ALL OF THEM CAN BE PRACTICED ON THE TRACKS

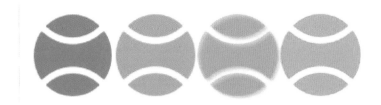

Orange ball stage
Warm-up

GAMES TO IMPROVE ON REACTION, COOPERATION AND SPATIAL AWARENESS

WARM-UP GAMES TO KEEP THEM ACTIVE AND ALERT

BALL TRACKING. RUN AFTER A BALL, CATCH IT, TOSS IT, PASS IT ON.

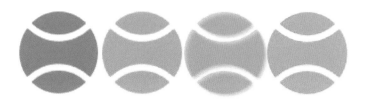

Orange ball stage
Activities

MAKE THE KIDS MOVE AND PUT THEIR ABILITIES TO TEST

GRADUALLY INCREASE THE DISTANCE BEWTWEEN PLAYERS AND WORK ON THEIR FOLLOW-THROUGH

COOPERATIVE PLAY. USE IT TO TRAIN LARGE GROUPS OF PLAYERS. ESPECIALLY WHEN EQUIPMENT IS LIMITED

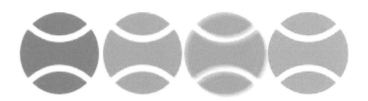

Orange ball stage
Activities

FOCUS ON
IMPROVING ONE
SHOT AT A TIME.
MAKE SURE THEY
HANDLE IT WELL
AND THEN MOVE ON
TO ANOTHER

INTRODUCE THE
PROPER BACKSWING
ONCE KIDS CONTROL
BALL AND DISTANCE

TEACH THEM ALL
SHOTS, THEIR
VARIATIONS AND
WHEN TO USE THEM

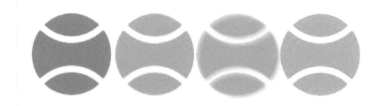

Orange ball stage
Activities

ALTERNATIVE EQUIPMENT CAN MAKE THE SESSION MORE EFFICIENT AND ENTERTAINING

SERVING PHASES: FOCUS ON GRIP AND PRONATION WITH PROGRESSIONS. A GOOD IMPACT BEFORE LEARNING THE FULL MOTION

TOWARDS THE END OF THIS STAGE, KIDS MUST DO ALL SHOTS WITH FULL SWING. TAKE BACK+CONTACT POINT+FOLLOW-THROUGH

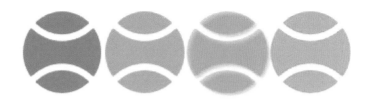

Orange ball stage
Activities

TACTICS AND COMPETITION SHOULD BE PRESENT IN EVERY SESSION. WATCH THEIR REACTIONS AS THEY PLAY

FAIR-PLAY, RESPECT, DISCIPLINE, TEAM SPIRIT. WE HAVE TO TEACH THEM TO INCORPORATE THAT TO THEIR EVERY-DAY BEHAVIOUR

TEAM COMPETITIONS CREATE A FRIENDLY AND RELAXED ENVIRONMENT AND INCREASE THE VALUE OF A TEAM

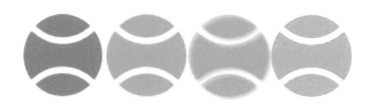

MINIPLAYERS TIPS

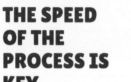

THE SPEED OF THE PROCESS IS KEY

GO SLOW AND MOVE ON SOLID GROUND

ESTABLISH A STRONG BASE IN EVERY ASPECT OF THE GAME

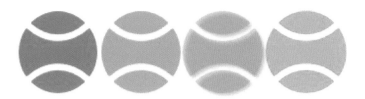

Orange ball stage
Conclusions

- This stage leads to a more technical approach to teaching-learning.
- Go slow. Once they processed what they are doing, move on to the next phase.
- Plenty of time to teach them all shots, movement and basic strategy knowledge.
- Competition should be relaxed, progressive. Team formats are the best option.

Green ball stage

Even though kids can play on full conventional court now, it is not a bad idea to keep them playing on a smaller court (orange) until most of the technical concepts are settled.
This is the best moment to teach them shots mechanics, movement, tactics, strategy and rules of the game to the detail as they are much more skillful and experienced.

Key points to have in mind:

- Kids can control their bodies better and if the previous process was accurate, we can define their playing personalities.
- Initiate them into competitions based on good technique, respectful behaviour and knowledge of the rules of the game.

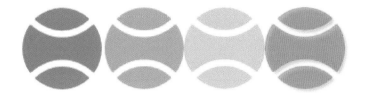

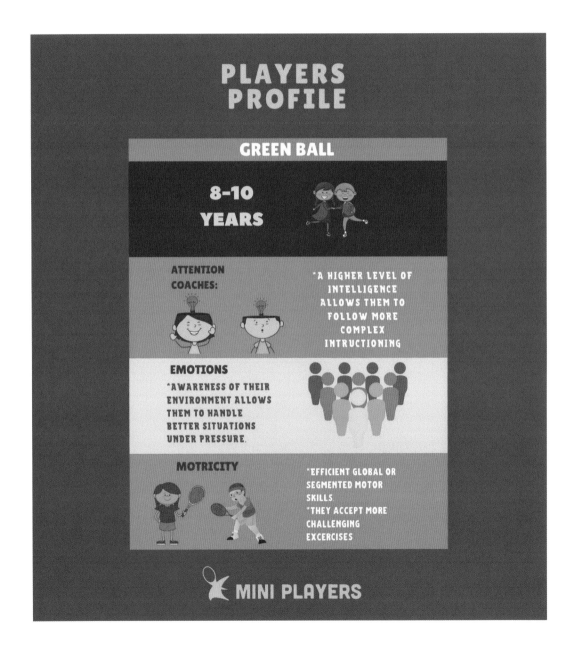

Green ball stage
Warm-up

SOFT TOUCHES. COORDINATED AND CONTROLLED RACKET SWING AND CONTACT

NATURAL AND FLUID MOVEMENT IS A MUST IN THIS STAGE

PRACTICE IN SMALL AREAS TO IMPROVE REACTION, DECISION MAKING AND RACKET CONTROL

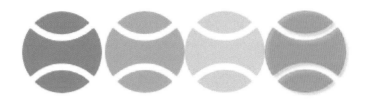

Green ball stage
Warm-up

ENHANCE THEIR POSITIONING BY WORKING ON BALANCE, ROTATIONS AND REACTION		
USE DRILLS ENVOLVING THE USE OF FEET BOTH ON AND OFF THE COURT		
SHOULDER ROTATION, PROPER FOOTWORK, BALL TRACKING. DON'T STOP WORKING ON THEM		

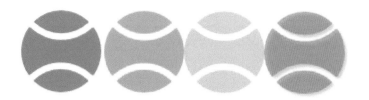

Green ball stage
Warm-up

FUNDAMENTALS! RUN, HIT, RECOVER, KEEP YOUR BALANCE!

STATIONS ALLOW COACHES TO WORK WITH MORE KIDS AND KEEP THEM ALL ACTIVE

SERVE: OPTIMIZE TECHNIQUE AND USE OF SPIN. MAKE THEM UNDERSTAND EVERY PHASE OF THE MOTION. PRECISION BEFORE POWER

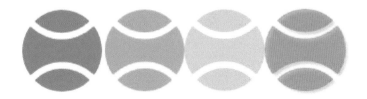

Green ball stage
Activities

IMPORTANCE OF CORRECT FOOTWORK AND STANCE. TEACH WORKING ROUTINES		
FINISHING THE POINT. TAKE THE INICIATIVE, CREATE THE SPACE AND GO FOR THE WINNER		
RETURN OF SERVE: PROGRESSIONS TO TEACH THEM RIGHT. BUILD AN AGGRESSIVE MENTALITY ON YOUR PLAYERS		

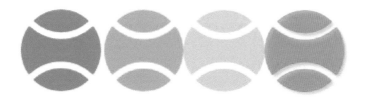

Green ball stage
Activities

PROPOSE SHORT AND DYNAMIC ROUTINES FOR PLAYERS DURING TRAINING

PRAISE TEAM SPIRIT WATCH THEIR MANNERS. FOCUS ON GROUP ACHIEVEMENTS

EFFORT CANNOT BE NEGOTIATED. THEY MUST GIVE THEIR BEST ALL THE TIME

Green ball stage
Activities

THEY MUST RESPECT COACHES, TEAMMATES, TASKS, EQUIPMENT, FACILITIES

US ALTERNATIVE METHODOLOGIES TO IMPROVE REACTION AND DECISION MAKING

INTRODUCTION TO COMPETITION SHOULD BE FUN AND FREE OF RESULTS/RANKING RELATED PRESSURE

Green ball stage
Activities

TRAINING SHOULD BE INTENSE, DYNAMIC AND DEMAND FULL CONCENTRATION

GROUP SESSIONS: SET UP STATIONS AND MAKE PROGRESSIONS ACCORDING TO THE TASKS. KEEP THEM BUSY AND ACTIVE

PLAYERS HAVE TO UNDERSTAND WHAT WE WANT FROM THEM. COACH THEM ACCORDINGLY

MINIPLAYERS TIPS

GLOBAL COMPREHENSION OF THE GAME

DETAILED SUPERVISION OF EVERY TECHNICAL GESTURE

GOOD BEHAVIOUR AND FAIR-PLAY AT ALL TIMES

RESPECT FOR COACHES, TEAMMATES, EQUIPMENT, FACILITIES AND THE GAME

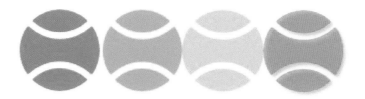

Green ball stage
Conclusions

- A coach in charge of groups of kids of this age should positively influence them, not only about technique and tactical information but also about social manners and behaviour.
- Once kids move on to Yellow ball, continue these training dynamics.
- Keep on working on coordination, they are still not fully aware of their own capabilities. Even well after this stage, they will experiment body changes, the length of their extremities, puberty.
- Pain in joints, sudden lack of coordination are some of the factors to have in mind when we prepare their training agenda.

Beyond blue, red, orange and green

BALANCE

SKILLS

ACTIVATION

TRANSFERRING

 **STATIONS**

 **RETURNS**

 **INSIDE OUT**

Inclusive tennis

How can we train kids and adults with intellectual disabilities?

Depending on the type of disability that people who wants to play tennis might have, we will have to adjust our methodology and the way we help them in their approach to the sport. For those with more serious coordination and mobility issues, the focus should be on familiarization with implements and a new space rather than technique.

How can we add inclusive tennis in our programmes?

Including tennis for the disabled as another part of the programme should always be considerd by tennis directors. In some cases, they can be introduced into some groups if the level of capabilities match. Events including people with disabilities become a great integration tool.

Can our players benefit from being part of inclusive events?

Working side by side with people who face on a daily basis all types of problems, limitations and physical issues and see them confronting them naturally, can be a great lesson for our players to open their eyes and push them to see life from a different perspective. Kids are very sensitive and they will learn from experiences that show them life in other conditions.

High performance training with disabled players

There are many players who reach high level of performance depending on the type discipline and competitions they are part of. There are all kind of competitions: *Special Olympics* for people with Down syndrome, wheelchair tennis tournaments, tennis for the blind, etc.
People are not used to see them in action and usually find it extremely surprising.

Is it posible to use the Mini Players style in their trainings?

No matter the level of disability, this style adapts perfectly to them.
Training patterns should be adapted according to the level of disabilities but the possibilities are endless.

High performance players can be trained in very demanding sessions following the basic ideas of this philosophy.

Proximity to players, focusing on actions control (shots, movement, balance, etc.) are exactly the same as any other players.

What kind of impact can tennis make on people with disabilities?

Practicing a sport, improving physical condition, avoining sedentarism, having a place where they can express themselves and relate to others.

Biggest impact is realizing they can play a sport and reinforce their self-esteem, fighting lack of motivation and depression, practicing outdoor (mainly) activities, getting to know new people and learning first hand the meaning of words like effort, discipline, team.

Adult groups

For those coaches who have worked with adult groups, these are the things they always demand:

- Dynamic.
- Lots of running, energetic-intense drills.
- A friendly environment.
- Playing competitive games.

What do we usually see in adult groups coaching?

Very common to see these 2 types:

1. A coach feeding ball nonstop to make them hit, run, pick-up and get back on the line, all of that at high intensity.
2. A session based on competitive games from minute 1.

Are these formats wrong?

No.

Can they be improved?

Of course they can.

We don´t have to forget that we must teach the sport the best way we can and our misión is to improve our players skills. So, we have to find the balance between a session with intensity and competition as adults always demand, but also, make corrections, work on their weaknesses and elevate their all-around game.

A good coach takes an active role, should always be kind and respectful, be completely involved in training and give them advices and information constantly.

A good way to handle an adult group is to set up friendly matches with players from other clubs and also organize extra training sessions on a weekend so they can get to play with others students.

This way, players feel they are part of an important group, see their coaches involved and integrated and you keep them valued and motivated.

Injury prevention

The most efficient measure to avoid injuries is to teach the best possible technique.

Frequent injuries in young players:

Incorrect technique

Bad postures, legs that never bend, dominant arm not fully extended at contact, unnecesary use of power, too much tension when holding the racket or not using the non-dominant hand to hold the racket when in ready position.

Incorrect grips

When kids lose control of their hands and start moving towards a Western grip, the power they must use to hit the ball over the net and gain some depth it is overwhealming. Too much pressure on the wrist and a bent arm open the door to future injuries. One-handed backhand players who don´t extend their dominant arm at contact and lead the swing with the elbow or two-handed backanders not using a Continental grip with the lower hand or hit with both hands separated will face lots of problems and their joints will suffer constantly.
Serving with an Eastern grip makes the elbow move in front of the body and lead the swing, generating power from a short, inefficient motion.

Inappropriate equipment

Some of the factors that can cause injuries due to incorrect use of equipment:

Rackets: using a bigger racket size than necessary is very common. Usually happens that a player is pushed to use a bigger racket to play full court or older kids because ¨he/she is better than the rest of his/her teammates¨.
The level of play is not the problem, but the physical and technical impact it is. Kids are not prepared to play lots of hours with heavier equipment. Even though their level can be much higher in their groups, they still have a lot to be learned and process shouldn´t be interrupted.

Balls: maybe the most painful mistake seeing in kids coaching. It is alarming to see that knowing that soft balls were created years ago, some coaches still don´t consider them as useful.

Using old yellow tennis balls with little kids it is completely wrong.

Even after losing some pressure, that ball is heavy for our youngest players who are using 21-23 inch rackets.

Reasons to use those balls are often heard between courts:

- "I learned that way".
- "It´s the same. They are old and they don´t bounce that much".
- "I have been using these balls all my life".
- "I don´t have enough budget to buy low-compression balls".
- "It´s better for them so they can get used to these balls".

All of these quotes, often said by experienced coaches, show the lack of correct policies in terms of teaching with proper equipment in many countries.

The equation is simple:

- Reduced tennis courts.
- Small and light rackets.
- Low-compression balls.

Excess of repetitions: depending on the training styles, large series of repetitions are part of daily routines.

The problem with this is that not always "more is better". We have to consider players in terms of age, intensity during sessions and rest periods.

When talking about 9/10-year-olds with a good level of tennis, they are put under heavy pressure because they get to be moved to groups with older kids, playing with yellow balls at a higher speed. Doing drills with repetitions can cause a traumatic stress on their joints, especially wrists, elbows, shoulders and knees.

Insufficient rest: let´s pretend we are talking about a 10-year-old kid who is going to school, has three training sessions per week, takes a private lesson on Saturday mornings, plays a singles tournament on Saturday afternoon and on Sunday plays a team´s competition, and it´s involved both in singles and doubles matches. This is nothing strange to witness nowadays. So the question would be: **When is this kid going to rest?** A general idea (urban legend?) says: ¨The more they play, the more they learn¨. This is correct, BUT if resting time is not considered part of the learning process, we are doing something very wrong.

Stress from school (lots of daily hours, exams, homework) plus the demands from practicing a sport (traingng intensity, results, rankings, unnecesary pressure, expectations) plus competitions on weekends, travelling, a quick meal between matches and so on. Not having proper rest leads to fatigue, lack of motivation-concentration, a lower level of performance, stress fractures.

Some final concepts

This book has tried to share ideas and experiences about the initiation to the game of tennis. Hopefuly they will help you to have more information about teaching young kids and make them love the sport once they practice it for the first time.

It is an open proposal that pushes people to create and discover new situations to teach and learn always having the focus on the players, no matter their level of skills and capacities.

The progression through stages, respecting kids' abilities and use of proper equipment suggests that cronological age shouldn't be the only criteria to make groups. We have to consider individual learning rythm, adaptability to tasks, personality and also make trainings enjoyable.

It is relevant as well the way coaches lead their groups. They should represent a model to be followed, someone who is there not only to improve their capacities but to help them interact, relate and feel part of a healthy environment.

This book also shows to leave an open door to integration and tennis promotion at all levels: values, solidarity spirit, support to different disadvantaged groups and, in the end, make a contribution to the integrity of our players.

With this chapter, this book ends, but not the will and desire to keep on learning and improving as coaches to have a positive influence on young people.

We honestly wish this book can help you to get new ideas or, at least, be more motivated when training.

You can follow us on social media and leave your comments!
They will be much appreciated.

Martin Rocca

Josep Campos-Rius

Bibliographic references

Avilés, C., Campos, A., & Abarca, J. P. (1996). *Estimulación y desarrollo en la iniciación al tenis*. Federación de Tenis de Chile.

Coyle, D. (2012). *The little book of talent: 52 tips for improving your skills*. Bantam.

Goodway, J. D., Ozmun, J. C., & Gallahue, D. L. (2019). *Understanding motor development: Infants, children, adolescents, adults*. Jones & Bartlett Learning.

Hammond, J., & Smith, C. (2006). Low compression tennis balls and skill development. *Journal of sports science & medicine, 5*(4), 575.

Kachel, K., Buszard, T., & Reid, M. (2015). The effect of ball compression on the match-play characteristics of elite junior tennis players. *Journal of sports sciences, 33*(3), 320-326.

Letort, O. (2002). *Tennis evolutif. Tennis cooleurs*. Champagnole: Editions Arts et literature.

Martínez, O. (2000). *Manual de formació psicopedagògica per a entrenadors d'iniciació esportiva*. Barcelona: Diputació de Barcelona.

Mowling, C. M., & Heidorn, B. (2013). Every shot counts: Rallying around traditional practice strategies. *Strategies, 26*(2), 30-36.

Muñoz, D., García, L., Timón, R., & Olcina, G. J. (2006). *Aprendizaje del tenis basado en la comprensión del juego*. II Congreso Nacional ciencias aplicadas al tenis, 18-20 mayo, Madrid.

Temple, V., & O'Connor, J. (2005). *HOP: Healthy Opportunities for Preschoolers: 1st Edition*. Vancouver Island Health Authority.

Complementary bibliography

Ahn, H., & Han, W. (2013). Objectivity of a measurement tool to evaluate the movements required to execute an effective flat serve at the tennis beginner's level. *The Korean Journal of Measurement and Evaluation in Physical Education and Sports Science, 15*(2), 17-28.

Allison, M. G., & Ayllon, T. (1980). Behavioral coaching in the development of skills in football, gymnastics, and tennis. *Journal of Applied Behavior Analysis, 13*, 297-314.

Antoun, R, & Thorp. D. (2011). *101 ejercicios de tenis para jóvenes*, Madrid: Tutor.

Aparicio, J. A., y Renes, V. M. (2016). *Las cualidades físicas en el tenis y su entrenamiento*. Madrid: Tutor.

Applewhaite, C. (2009). *Mejora tu tenis*. Barcelona: Paidotribo.

Aznar, R. (2011). *Intervención docente en la enseñanza de los deportes de raqueta en educación física a través de una investigación-acción*. Tesis Doctoral, Universidad de Valencia: Valencia.

Aznar, R. (2014). *Los deportes de raqueta: Modalidades lúdico-deportivas con diferentes implementos*. Barcelona: Inde.

Barrell, M. (2013). Do you get me? Strategies to create learning in Tennis10s! *Coaching & Sport Science Review, 60*, 21–23.

Bollettieri, N. (2001). *Bollettieri's Tennis Handbook*. Champaign, EEUU: Human Kinetics.

Buszard, T., Reid, M., Masters, R., & Farrow, D. (2016). Scaling Tennis During PE in Primary School to Enhance Motor Skill Acquisition. *Research Quarterly for Exercise and Sport, 87* (4), 414-420.

Carreras, J. C., y Gímenez, J. (2010). Metodología de enseñanza utilizada en la enseñanza del tenis durante la etapa de iniciación. *Retos. Nuevas tendencias en Educación Física, Deporte y Recreación, 18*, 60-65.

Casey, A., & Dyson, B. (2010). The implementation of models-based practice in physical education trough action research. *European Physical Education Review, 15*(2), 175-199.

Chang-Keun, C., Park, J., Park, D., & Lee, J. (2009). The Process of How Elementary School Teachers adapt to In-service Tennis Training. *The Korean Journal of Elementary Physical Education, 15*(1), 105-120.

Contreras, O., García, L. M., Gutiérrez, D., Del Valle, S., y Aceña, R. M. (2007). *Iniciación a los deportes de raqueta. La enseñanza de los deportes de red y muro desde un enfoque constructivista*. Barcelona: Paidotribo.

Courel, J., & Sánchez-Alcaraz, B. J. (2017). Teaching tennis by means of a constructivist approach. *ITF Coaching and Sport Science Review, 71*(25), 20-22.

Cramier, J. (2004). L'evolution de l'enseignement. *EPS Education Physique & Sport, 307*, 22–24.

Crespo, M. (1999). *Being a better tennis parent*. London: International Tennis Federation.

Crespo, M. (2001). *Manual sobre formatos de competición*. Londres: ITF. International Tennis Federation.

Crespo, M. (2001). *The tennis volunteer*. London: International Tennis Federation.

Crespo, M. (2002). *Entrenamiento de tenistas iniciantes e intermedios*. Londres: ITF. International Tennis Federation.

Crespo, M. (2002). *Trabajando con jóvenes tenistas*. Londres: ITF. International Tennis Federation.

Crespo, M. (2006). Nuevas perspectivas en la investigación y aplicación al tenis. *Congreso Mundial de Deportes de Raqueta*, Madrid.

Crespo, M. (2006). *Tennis psychology*. London: International Tennis Federation.

Crespo, M., Pluim, B., & Reid, M. (2001). *Tennis medicine for tennis coaches*. London: International Tennis Federation.

Crespo, M., Reid, M. M., & Miley, D. (2004). Tennis: Applied examples of a game-based teaching approach. *Strategies, 17*(4), 27-30.

Crespo, M., Reid, M., & Miley, D. (2004). Tennis: Applied examples of a game-based teaching approach. *Strategies: A Journal for Physical Education and Sport Educators, 17*(4), 27-30. doi: 10.1080/08924562.2004.10591100

Cutton, D. M., & Landin, D. (2007). The effects of self-talk and augmented feedback on learning the tennis forehand. *Journal of Applied Sport Psychology, 19*(3), 288-303. DOI: 10.1080/10413200701328664

Davies, K., y Van Wyk, J. (2009). El negocio del tenis: Promoción de programas de tenis en clubes y federaciones para tenistas de todos los niveles de juego II. *ITF Coaching and Sport Science Review, 48*, 13.

Dillard, K. (2003). Using key words to develop sport skills. *Strategies, 17*(2), 32–34.

Douvis, S. J. (2005). Variable practice in learning the forehand drive in tennis. *Perceptual and Motor Skills, 101*(2), 531-545.

Efran, J. S., Lesser, G. S. y Spiller, M. J. (1994). Enhancing tennis coaching with youths using a metaphor method. *Sport Psychologist, 8*(4), 349-359.

Elderton, W. (2008). Situation Training: Key to Training in a Game-based Approach. *Coaching & Sport Science Review, 44*, 24–25.

Elderton, W. (2009). Tenis progresivo: Desarrollo de 5 a 7 años de edad. *ITF Coaching & Sport Science Review, 16*(47), 5-6.

Elderton, W. (2013). Principles of modern coaching methodology: An evolution. *Coaching & Sport Science Review, 60*, 9–11.

Elliot, B., Reid, M., & Crespo, M. (2009). *Technique development in tennis stroke production*. London: International Tennis Federation.

Elliott, B. (2006). Biomechanics and tennis. *British Journal of Sports Medicine, 40*, 392–396.

Ene-Voiculescu, C., & Ene-Voiculescu, V. (2010). Methodology of Training for Developing Young Tennis Players (Aged 10 - 12 Years Old). *Ovidius University Annals, Series Physical Education & Sport/Science, Movement & Health, 10*(2), 484–485.

Faber, I. R., Bustin, P. M. J., Oosterveld, F. G. J., Elferink-Gemser, M. T., & Nijhuis-Van der Sanden, M. W. G. (2016). Assessing personal talent determinants in young racquet sport players: a systematic review. *Journal of Sports Sciences, 34*(5), 395–410.

Farrow, D., & Maschette, W. (1997). The effects of contextual interference on children learning forehand tennis groundstrokes. *Journal of Human Movement Studies, 33*(2), 47-67.

Federación Internacional de Tenis (1995). *Manual para entrenadores*. Londres: ITF.

Federación Internacional de Tenis (1998). *Iniciativa de la ITF del tenis en las escuelas*. Londres:

ITF.

Fernández-Fernández, J., Méndez, A., y Sanz, D. (2012). *Fundamentos del entrenamiento de la condición física para jugadores de tenis en formación.* Barcelona: Real Federación Española de Tenis.

Fitzpatrick, A., Davids, K., & Stone, J. A. (2017). Effects of Lawn Tennis Association mini tennis as task constraints on children's match-play characteristics. *Journal of Sports Sciences, 35*(22), 2204–2210.

Fitzpatrick, A., Davids, K., & Stone, J. A. (2018). Effects of an 8-week mini tennis coaching intervention on children's groundstroke performance. *Coaching & Sport Science Review, 76,* 9–11.

Fitzpatrick, A., Davids, K., & Stone, J. A. (2018). Effects of scaling task constraints on emergent behaviours in children's racquet sports performance. *Human Movement Science, 58,* 80–87.

Fitzpatrick, A., Davids, K., & Stone, J. A. (2018). How do LTA mini tennis modifications shape children's match-play performance? *Coaching & Sport Science Review, 74,* 3–5.

Flick, L. (2020). Ten and Under Tennis for ALL Ages! *JOPERD: The Journal of Physical Education, Recreation & Dance, 91*(4), 46–48.

Fry, M. D., & Newton, M. (2003). Application of achievement goal theory in an urban youth tennis setting. *Journal of Applied Sport Psychology, 15*(1), 50-66.

García-González, L., Moreno, A., Gil, A., Moreno, M. P., & Villar, F. D. (2014). Effects of Decision Training on Decision Making and Performance in Young Tennis Players: An Applied Research. *Journal of Applied Sport Psychology, 26*(4), 426–440.

Gómez, M. M. (2015). Coaching developing players, "a view from the ecological approach." *Coaching & Sport Science Review, 65,* 16–18.

Gonzalez, R. (2012). Tenis 10s: El cambio de reglas conlleva un ajuste metodológico. *Coaching & Sport Science Review, 57,* 23–27.

Guillot, A., Desliens, S., Rouyer, C., & Rogowski, I. (2013). Motor imagery and tennis serve performance: The external focus efficacy. *Journal of Sports Science and Medicine, 12,* 332-338.

Hebert, E. P., & Landin, D. (1994). Effects of a learning model and augmented feedback on tennis skill acquisition. *Research Quarterly for Exercise and Sport, 65*(3), 250-257.

Hebert, E. P., Landin, D., & Solmon, M. A. (2004). The impact of task progressions on college students' skill achievement in tennis. *Journal of Human Movement Studies, 46*(3), 227-248.

Helfrich, J. (2006). Teaching and Coaching Tennis Using System 5. *Strategies, 20*(2), 7–13.

Hernández, M. (1998). *Deportes de raqueta.* Madrid: Ministerio de Educación y Cultura. Consejo Superior de Deportes.

Hulteen, R., Lander, N., Morgan, P., Barnett, L., Robertson, S., & Lubans, D. (2015). Validity and Reliability of Field-Based Measures for Assessing Movement Skill Competency in Lifelong Physical Activities: A Systematic Review. *Sports Medicine, 45*(10), 1443–1454.

Ioannis, A., Athanasios, L., & Gioros, Z. (2015). The educational system of coaching schools in tennis. The case of Greece. *Journal of Physical Education & Sport, 15*(2), 208–211.

Iserbyt, P., Madou, B., Vergauwen, L., & Behets, D. (2011). Effects of Peer Mediated Instruction with Task Cards on Motor Skill Acquisition in Tennis. *Journal of Teaching in Physical Education, 30*(1), 31-50.

Kalapoda, E., Michalopoulou, M., Aggelousis, N., & Taxildaris, K. (2003). Discovery learning and modelling when learning skills in tennis. *Journal of Human Movement Studies, 45*(5), 433-448.

Kim, S., & Yu, Y. (2009). A teaching method for serve skill betterment of tennis beginners. *Journal of Sport and Leisure Studies, 37*, 137-147.

Lameiras, J., de Almeida, P. L., & Garcia-Mas, A. (2015). La eficacia de la metodología old way/ new way en la corrección de un error técnico automatizado y su impacto en las habilidades psicológicas del atleta: estudio de caso en el tenis. *Cuadernos de Psicología Del Deporte, 15*(2), 79–85.

Le Pallec, A., & Guinard, J. Y. (2008). Distance entre productions didactiques et pratiques compétitives: un exemple en didactique du tennis. *Movement & Sport Sciences, 65*, 57-77.

Lewis, F. R., Knight, C. J., & Mellalieu, S. D. (2017). Emotional experiences in youth tennis. *Psychology of Sport & Exercise, 29*, 69–83.

Luiz Corrêa, M. M., Rodrigues Freitas, T. C., & Aparecida da Silva, S. (2019). The teaching of racket sports in the school environment. *Caderno de Educação Física e Esporte, 17*(1), 309–316.

Matikova -Tamburova, S. (2013). Methodological Guidelines for Initial Traninig in Techniques and Tactics of Tennis. *Activities in Physical Education & Sport, 3*(1), 132–134.

McPherson, S. L., & Thomas, J. R. (1989). Relation of knowledge and performance in boys' tennis: age and expertise. *Journal of Experimental Child Psychology, 48*, 190-211

Miley, D. (2017). How to better introduce and retain recreational adult tennis players in tennis the best sport for life, general health and fitness. *Coaching & Sport Science Review, 72*, 21–23.

Miller, S. (Ed.) (2003). *Tennis science and Technology*. Oxford: Blackwell science.

Miranda, M. (2001). Mini-tennis: being on time for the tennis lesson. *Coaching & Sport Science Review, 25*, 11.

Miranda, M. (2002). Cómo utilizar el mini-tenis de forma eficaz. *ITF Coaching & Sport Science Review, 10*(26), 11-13.

Miranda, M. (2015). The trajectory as the basis of tactics: Basic work on red courts. *Coaching*

& Sport Science Review, *65*, 24–25.

Momchilova, A., & Neikov, I. (2012). Communication Skills of the Teacher - Factor for Effective Training in Tennis in the Hours of Sports Games. *Research in Kinesiology*, *40*(1), 3–8.

Moreno, F. J., Luís, V., Menayo, R. y Fuentes, J. P. (2009). *Bases del control y del aprendizaje aplicadas al tenis*. Sevilla: Wanceulen.

Murray, J. F. (2002). *Tenis inteligente*. Barcelona: Paidotribo.

Neuman, M. C., & Singer, R. N. (1968). A comparison of traditional versus programed methods of learning tennis. *Research Quarterly*, *39*(4), 1044-1048.

Ortiz, R. H. (2004). *Tenis: Potencia, velocidad y movilidad*. Barcelona: Inde.

Papageorgaki, Z. K., & Dramitinos, A. (2016). Mini-Tennis for Children and Parents. *Physical Education Matters*, *11*(2), 38–39.

Park, S. (2009). Applications of blended learning for tennis practical learning. *The Korean Society of Sports Science*, *18*(3), 479-490.

Pinho, J. (2019). Creating Your Teaching Methodology. *Addvantage*, *47*(3), 51–52.

Pluim, B. M., Groppel, J. L., Miley, D., Crespo, M., & Turner, M. S. (2018). Health benefits of tennis. *British Journal of Sports Medicine, 52*(3), 201-202.

Reid, M., Quinn, A., & Crespo, M. (2003). *Strength and conditioning for tennis*. London: International Tennis Federation.

Reid, M., Quinn, A., & Crespo, M. (2010). *Fuerza y condición física para el tenis*. Londres: ITF. International Tennis Federation.

Renström, A.F.H. (Ed.). (2002). *Tennis*. Oxford: Blackwell science.

Roetert, E. P. y Kovacs, M. S. (2012). *Anatomía del tenista: Guía ilustrada para mejorar la fuerza, la velocidad, la potencia y la agilidad del tenista*. Madrid: Tutor.

Roetert, E. P., & Lubbers, P. (2011). The role of sport science in coaching education. *Coaching & Sport Science Review*, *54*, 5–6.

Rowland, T. W. (2015). *La ciencia del tenis: cómo influyen los factores psicológicos, fisiológicos y físicos en el dominio de la pista*. Madrid: Tutor.

Ruiz, A., y Ferragut, C. (2011). *Deportes de raqueta*. Madrid: Gymnos.

Rutherford, J. (2017). *Skills, Drills & Strategies for Tennis*. New York: Routledge.

Sahan A., Erman K. A., & Ertekin E. (2018). The effect of a variable practice method on tennis groundstroke learning of adult beginners. *Coaching & Sport Science Review*, *74*, 15–17.

Sánchez, Alcaraz, B. J. (2016). *Deportes de raqueta y pala: claves para su enseñanza*. Madrid: Pila Teleña.

Sánchez-Alcaraz, B. J. (2013). Principios para la enseñanza del mini-tenis en la escuela. *Trances:*

Revista de Transmisión del Conocimiento Educativo y de la Salud, 5(2), 177-186.

Sanz, D. (2003). *El tenis en silla de ruedas. De la iniciación a la competición*. Barcelona: Paidotribo.

Sanz, D. (2012). Variability during training sessions to develop coordination skills in the development of tennis players. *Coaching & Sport Science Review, 58*, 16–18.

Sanz, D. (2017). The importance of modifying the equipment for beginner tennis players: Tennis Play and Stay development in Spain. *Coaching & Sport Science Review, 72*, 8–9.

Schönborn, R. (1999). *Tenis*. Madrid: Tutor.

Smeeton, N. J., Huys, R., & Jacobs, D. M. (2013). When less is more: Reduced usefulness training for the learning of anticipation skill in tennis. *Plos One, 8*(11). DOI: 10.1371/journal.pone.0079811

Solanellas, F., Morejon, S., & Campos, J. (2000). *I ara, tennis!!! El tennis als centres d'ensenyament*. Barcelona: Federació Catalana de Tennis.

Tennant, M. (2002). Mini-tennis: appropriate competition for mini tennis. *Coaching & Sport Science Review, 28*, 10–11.

Tennant, M. (2005). *Manual de Play Tennis*. Londres: ITF. International Tennis Federation.

Tennant, M. (2013). Principles of adult learning. *Coaching & Sport Science Review, 60*, 18–20.

The modern approach to mini-tennis. (2015). *Coaching & Sport Science Review, 66*, 9–10.

Tomov, D., & Ivanov, S. (2012). Methodology of Teaching and Training Tennis in Classes of Physical Education at Higher Schools. *Activities in Physical Education & Sport, 2*(1), 57–61.

Torres, G., y Carrasco, L. (2005). *El tenis en la escuela*. Barcelona: Inde.

Turner, A., & Martinek, T. J. (1995). Teaching for understanding: A model for improving decision making during game play. *Quest, 47*(1), 44-63.

Turner, A., Crespo, M., Reid, M., & Miley, D. (2002). The games for understanding (GFU) teaching approach in tennis. *Coaching & Sport Science Review, 26*, 2–3.

Unierzyski, P., & Crespo, M. (2007). Review of modern teaching methods for tennis. *RICYDE. Revista Internacional de Ciencias del Deporte, 3*(7), 1-10.

Unierzyski, P., Bogusławski, M., & Wheatley, S. (2018). Applied Integrated training on-court - specific case studies: Is it a methodology of the future? *Coaching & Sport Science Review, 75*, 31–33.

Van Daalen, M. (2011). *Teaching Tennis Volume 1: The Fundamentals of the Game (For Coaches, Players, and Parents)* (Vol. 1). Bloomington: Xlibris Corporation.

Vesseaux, L. (2003). Mini-tennis: recommending tennis equipment. *Coaching & Sport Science Review, 29*, 10–11.

Watanabe, D. (1978). An explanation paradigm for tennis instruction: A different point of view. *International Journal of Sport Psychology, 9*(1), 53-54.

White, S. (2007). *Teaching Tennis - From Tots to Teen: The Complete Guide for Parents & Coaches.* Rockville, MD: Arc Manor.

Wiezel, A., & Kulahci, M. (2004). Sensitivity of tennis players to racquet characteristics. *Engineering of Sport 5, Volume 1, 1,* 458–464.

Williams, A. M., Ward, P., Allen. D., & Smeeton, N. J. (2004). Developing anticipation skills in tennis using on-court instruction: perception versus perception and action. *Journal of Applied Sport Psychology, 16,* 350-360.

Wilson, D. (2009). The Game-Based Coaching Methodology - An Investigation of Principles and Practice. *Coaching & Sport Science Review, 49,* 19–20.

Zetou, E., Koronas, V., Athanailidis, I., & Koussis, P. (2012). Learning tennis skill through game Play and Stay in elementary pupils. *Journal of Human Sport and Exercise, 7*(2), 560-572.

Printed in Great Britain
by Amazon